A BEAM OF LIGHT IN A DARK PLACE

Dainah Garth Felton

Copyright © 2013 Dainah Garth Felton
Original Copyright 2004   TXu 1-193-217

All rights reserved. No part of this book may be reproduced in any form or by any means, electronic or mechanical, including photocopying, recording, or by any information storage and retrieval system, without written permission from the author. This excludes a reviewer who may quote brief passages in a review. Unless otherwise noted, all Scripture quotations are from The Holy Bible, King James Version (KJV)

Library of Congress
Cataloging-in-Publication Data
   Felton, Dainah Garth
   Religion: Inspirational

Photographer: Keith L. Spiller Jr.
Cover Design: Brittany J. Jackson
Published by G Publishing, LLC

Library of Congress Control Number:
    2013937816
ISBN: 978-0-9883374-4-2
Printed in the United States of America

DEDICATION

I dedicate this book to my parents, Jesse and Elizabeth Garth. They are the fiber of our family. My mom is still here with us. God has blessed her down through the years. She is a beautiful woman. My dad passed away in December 2001. He was a handsome and very strong man, a man that was not a stranger to hard work.

He had a large pair of gifted hands. In his spare time he would build and fix things, make things, paint, plant beautiful gardens, and he was an excellent coooo'k. You couldn't put my mom and dad in kitchen at the same time, there would be too many delicious dishes to choose from.

Thank you for my Parents Lord, Jesse and Elizabeth Garth. They will forever hold a special place in our hearts. Both now and forever.

ACKNOWLEDGMENTS

I would like to thank my husband Tim for his encouragement, support and love. I also would like to thank my former pastor, and father in the gospel, District Elder Claude Allen Jr. for his countless hours of prayer for me as well as his encouraging support.

A special thank you to Ke-Ke Cheese, my inspiration and chip off the old block. Roll over Beethoven and tell Tchaikovsky the news! To my niece Jazze, I thank you for your precious time and wonderful help. A large thank you to my spiritual family as well as my natural family for all that you have been to me.

TABLE OF CONTENTS

PREFACE vii

INTRODUCTION ix

CHAPTER ONE: DIRECTION 12

CHAPTER TWO: CAN THE STORMS BE WEATHERED............................ 18

CHAPTER THREE: GOD'S PEOPLE.................. 24

CHAPTER FOUR: FINDING WHAT WAS MINE 30

CHAPTER FIVE: RECEVING WHAT WAS MINE 42

CHAPTER SIX: KEEPING WHAT IS MINE...... 52

CHAPTER SEVEN: MY EXCEEDING AND GREAT REWARD... 58

CHAPTER EIGHT: FAITH 64

FAITH: THE POEM.. 70

ABOUT THE AUTHOR 74

PREFACE

The Lord inspired "A BEAM OF LIGHT IN A DARK PLACE" in my spirit when He came into my life. He deals with His people according to His good pleasure. He uses us in our own character to do an appointed work.

I praise Him for allowing me to testify of His soul healing, wonderful life transforming, mind altering, and regeneration of the living dead.

I praise Him for knowing, we can cling to that old rugged cross and exchange it someday for a crown......

"Just Over The Hill Side"

I have a mortgage free mansion custom designed with Dainah Garth Felton exclusively in mind…
Where the brilliant bright, is brighter than sun light, and darkness will never roam……

This place has been prepared for me, by my Heavenly Father. It will throughout all eternity forever be my home.
"Just Over The Hill Side"

INTRODUCTION

My intentions in writing this book is to display the "FAITH" that the love of God instills in your heart, to witness to a lost and dying world and to encourage the saints of God to continue to hold fast to Gods unchanging hand.

"I am God, and there is none else:"
"I am God, and there is none like me.
declaring the end from the beginning, and from ancient times the things that are not yet done, saying my counsel stand and I will do all my pleasure:"
(Isaiah 46:9-10)

CHAPTER ONE: DIRECTION

CHAPTER ONE: DIRECTION

When you don't know Jesus you try to plan your life on your own. Just living one day at a time, no real sense of direction. I was just kind of walking through a hazy fog, wanting something better out of life.

A normal childhood doing things of the world is how I grew up. No spiritual direction, only knowing that there was a God. As a child I remember doing things that were nice and feeling good about them. I also remember doing things that were not so nice and feeling bad about them. I remember getting down on my knees to pray as a child, even though no one told me that I should. There was always a part of me that always wanted to be good. I had a funny kind of character, I was always being misunderstood.

As I look back over my life, growing up was fun, I did basically the normal things, you know giggly girlfriends and little boyfriends along the way. When I was fourteen years old I went on my first significant trip.

It was a two week vacation to visit my grandparents in Alabama. One of the main events that stick out in my mind was the framed picture that I brought my sister back as a gift. It was a picture of Jesus in the Garden of Gethsemane. I had no idea that Jesus had a calling on my life, and that one day in the future I would be preaching the good news gospel.

When I gave my sister that picture it had very little significance to me at all. It was just a gift, as a matter of a fact. I didn't even know what the picture represented. I just thought it was a picture portraying Jesus on his knees praying on a rock.

As I look back on that time in my life I realize that it was at that particular setting that Jesus was praying to the father that His will be done in Him. He would die on the cross for the sins of the world, that we could have eternal life. I believe that, that gift purchased at that moment in time was for a reason. It certainly helped me to realize even more today that Jesus had a plan for my life even when I didn't truly know who He was. God has a way of bringing to our remembrance that He was there all the time, even when we did not realize it.

My sister still has that picture today and that event took place over 45 years ago. What a mighty God we serve, He is a true and constant friend.

By the time I was 24 I craved for a place where I could get to know God. So I began to join different churches. Without any guidance, I kind of just wondered in and out of churches until I completely stopped going. I found nothing that would hold my interest there. Perhaps I really didn't know for sure what I was interested in.

I know for myself, with experience, and assurance that the Lord will trouble your heart and allow things to come into your life to get you right at the brink of yielding your life unto him. When you have shown yielding signs for Him in your life, He will come.

"Verily, verily, I say unto you, He that believeth on me, the works that I do shall he do also; and greater

works than these shall he do;
because I go unto my Father.
And whatsoever ye shall ask in my
name, that will I do, that the Father
may be glorified in the Son.
If ye shall ask any thing in my name,
I will do it."
(St. John 14:12-14)

CHAPTER TWO: CAN THE STORMS BE WEATHERED

CHAPTER TWO: CAN THE STORMS BE WEATHERED

After going through a very rocky plain, and the word rocky I found to be more than just a catchy phrase. It does literally mean going through some pretty stony and unleveled areas without shoes on so to speak. I went through some very heart wrenching painful times.

The more I went through, the more I began to pray. You see, no one believes that you should have an easy carefree, good, productive, meaningful life more than yourself. So I began what I will call my, "Clean up Crusade."

This is where I went into the mold of trying to clean up my life all by myself, without the power of God, being the center of my joy. When you draw nigh unto God He will draw nigh unto you.

> "There is something about God's
> GRACE
> He will stand you in front of a mirror of truth and allow you to focus on what you need to face"

The first thing I did was desire to stop drinking and to stop smoking. I knew that those things were no good for me even though I liked doing them. I through that God would be pleased with that and He was because, He blessed me in that with some supernatural power. For a very long time those two things had taken a deep root in my life and it was only by His grace that I was able to stop. It was not a long drawn out "Try and Try again" process. When the Lord gave me grace I was able to stop one right after the other in a blink of an eye, with not a desire to start back up again.

God took away my drinking of alcohol in the month of May 1989, next it was the smoking in August of 1989. He took those taste right out of my mouth, there was no withdraw symptoms or detoxifying, just the precious grace of God.

After the Lord had blessed me in that manner, "My FAITH" began to increase because; I knew that it was God that had blessed me in my victory over those two strong holds.

> "Faith is the substance of things Hoped for and the evidence of things not seen." Heb. 11:1
>
> It affords you the ability to step out into the unknown without a plan just trusting Jesus alone…….

God had now shown Himself to me in a personal manner, the more the Lord revealed Himself to me the more I began to realize that this

God that I had just heard about was really real. "MY FAITH" began to sprout wings.

When you have come to a place where you truly believe that God is real. He will take you from "FAITH to FAITH" and from "STRENGTH to STRENGTH." He is a rewarder of those who diligently seek Him. I sought the Lord and He heard my cry. He began to place people in my life that would help me to find the road to redemption Thank You Lord.

> "But rather seek ye the kingdom of God; and all these things shall be added unto you."
> (St. Luke 12:31)

CHAPTER THREE: GOD'S PEOPLE

CHAPTER THREE: GOD'S PEOPLE

When nothing else would help, love lifted me..........

"Charity suffereth long and is kind; charity envieth not; vaunteth not itself,
is not puffed up. Doth not behave itself
unseemly, seeketh not her own, is not easily provoked thinketh no evil,
rejoiceth not in iniquity, but rejoiceth in truth."
(1st Corinth. 13:4-6)

As the people that God had assigned to come into my life to minister to me began to come they were soothing to my heart and my mind, but my flesh still wanted to reject them. There were some things that I had given up, and there were some things that I was still holding on to. What I needed was some overcoming power.

Where would I get that from? In the natural who would be so brave as to be excited about walking into the unknown.

> "Be careful for nothing but in everything by prayer and supplication with thanksgiving let your request be made known unto God. And the peace of God, which passeth all understanding, shall keep your hearts and minds through Christ Jesus."
> (Philip. 4:6-7)

Yet I continued to feel a strong need for God in my life. The people that He had sent would give me just a little bit of His word at a time, so that I could crave, eat and digest the bread of life.

For a while I just went on, day after day on what I thought to be my own strength. Some things I had the power to turn away from and some things still had power over me. They were not hard core things like drugs and riotous living but, simpler things such as dancing and secular music. I could really get into the lyrics of music and apply them to what I wanted or what I didn't want in my life. And when I look at it now those types of strongholds in my life was nothing but emptiness and time consuming, oh how precious time is. Time is the one thing that you cannot store away for future use.

The people of God must have been putting tenderizer on the words God had given then to minister to me because, my heart began to become more and more tender and receptive to what I was hearing.

While I was hearing I was also seeing a way of life from these people that was very different from my own. They had some sense of peace and joy about them that caused them to have a calm, and they appeared to be happy all the time I noticed that they didn't act and react to things the way most people did.

> "To everything there is a season,
> and a time to every purpose
> under the heaven."
> (Eccles. 3:1)

For every person in life there is a reason….

What did they have that I didn't have? It wasn't anything that was material that the eye could see and I could work toward getting like a trophy. It was a way of life that they lived that appeared to be clean, fresh and wholesome. "What was that?"

CHAPTER FOUR: FINDING WHAT WAS MINE

CHAPTER FOUR: FINDING WHAT WAS MINE

Well, I struck out with some new found determination to find out what I had to do to get that peace and calm and that focus in my life. There are so many elements as we live our lives out in this cold world that will detour us from having a God led focus.

I began to talk to God's people in detail about what I wanted, and they responded with loving cords, drawing me to a place where I could receive the Lord into my life, and know with assurance that Jesus could be mine. We continued to talk and my heart began to long for Jesus in a way that I had never known.

"Come unto me all ye that labor

And are heavy laden and I will give you rest. Take my yoke upon you, and learn of me; for I am meek and lowly in heart; and ye shall find rest unto your souls. For my yoke is easy and my burden is light."
(St. Matt. 11:28)

Jesus knows how to get your Attention and His timing is always right..........

One day I walked into the presence of one of the people that the lord had put in my life. I began to tell this person I wanted to be saved, and their ears were opened to me as always. I truly felt like it was time for me to make a change.

"When a man's ways please the Lord, He maketh even his enemies to be at peace with him. Better is a little with righteousness than great revenues without right. A man's

> heart deviseth His way: but the Lord
> directeth his steps.
> (Prov. 16:7-9)

I continued on with what I had purposed in my mind, sharing my life with a great genuine sincerity. To close out the conversation I told them that I wanted to come over to their church the following Sunday to be baptized, I meant it with all my heart. You see I thought if I got baptized that would make me clean as I needed to be, to be accepted by God.

All of a sudden I had this certain new feeling of independence; as if I was being led by a soothing force to do something good with my life, something better. Later on in the day after that fearless force had kind of subsided, I began to wonder and worry about what my family and friends would say if I told them about my plan to be totally committed to the Lord.

It was a bit frightening to me because I didn't know too much about what I was doing, it just felt right. I didn't know what to expect or what not to expect.

People of the world really don't have a problem with you when you are just going to church and nothing seems to change in your life. Oh, but when you begin to go to church and stop doing the things you use to do, and there is a noticeable difference in your life, you are going to run into some trouble. And that's exactly what happened to me. People began to persecute and mistreat me and even tried to make me feel ridiculous about the decisions I had made by God's grace, Just to name a few of the obstacles that I faced head on.

"But they that wait upon the Lord
Shall renew their strength; they
Shall mount up with wings as eagles;
They shall run and not be weary; and
They shall walk and not faint."
(Isaiah 4:31)

These are the people that go on to be Gods saints............

I had gotten this made up mind from somewhere that I was going to seek the Lord while He may be found. So I casted aside the worry and doubt, and just became less concerned about what everybody was going to do or say, I didn't even know what I was going to do or say, or even what that was supposed to be. The Lord said in His word, cast all your cares upon me for I care for you.

When that Sunday came, I woke up with a wonderful burst of energy and a very strong determination, I was determined to get myself over to this church where I thought I could find some new hope, after I got there I didn't know what was going to happen, what I did know was that I was ready for it to happen. I had not tried to rehearse anything; I had no idea what I was going to say. I was home alone that particular day, with a made up mind.

Well, me myself and I got up, got myself together, got in the car and headed toward the church. That's when the Lord took over. I did no resisting I just allowed the Lord to lead me.

> "Trust in the Lord with all thine heart and lean not unto thine own understanding. In all thy ways acknowledge Him and He

shall direct thy path."
Prov. 3:5-6

When you allow God to direct
Your path He will give you rest
In the aftermath………..

I had been to this church before, but that morning the Lord led me in a totally different direction.

Before I knew anything I looked up to my left and there was the church sitting right on the corner where it had always sat. I was looking at it from a different angle and mind set.

I went inside the church and some of the people remembered me from previous visits. I went in and kind of sat toward the back, and people kept asking me did I want to go up closer to the front where I had friends sitting, Or if I wanted them to let my friends know that I was there. My answer was no because, I truly didn't come to visit.

Service began, the choir sang, and then the announcer came with the announcements for the week, after which she asked if there were any visitors. I stood to my feet and with a very bold voice that had to have come from the Lord because; I was always uncomfortable speaking in front of a lot of people.

I had this uncontrollable shake that would become more intense and flare up whenever I tried to speak in front of people. There was a spirit of fear that would hover over me which was a weight that I carried around, up until this point my whole life. I gave them my name and then I told the congregation that I had some very dear friends there, but I did not come to visit. It was then that I was just overtaken by some type of commitment to become closer to God.

As tears began to stream down my face I stood there and I began to tell them that I was there because I wanted to be baptized in Jesus name and receive the precious gift of the Holy Ghost that day.

> "For God hath not given us a spirit
> Of fear but of power and love, and
> Of a sound mind."
> (2nd Tim. 1:7)

The power and love of God is very kind. After I finished talking I just stood there again, I didn't know what was going to happen next. One of the ministers began to speak from the pulpit, I will never forget his words, he said that they needed to stop what they were doing and prepare this young lady to be baptized in Jesus name.

In the middle of service they actually took me to the baptismal room and, prepared me to be baptized, and talked to me about what I must do to be saved. As I listened and went over scripture with them so that I would understand what I was about to do, I suddenly realized that I had already began preparing to be born again.

When I allowed the Lord to lead me to that church that day. I also began to realize that when I stood up and announced that I wanted to be baptized in Jesus name with tears streaming down my face that I had already began to repent in my heart.

"Then Peter said unto them, repent, And be baptized every one of you in the name of Jesus Christ for the remission of sins, and ye shall receive the gift of the Holy Ghost.

For the promise is unto you and to your children and to all that are afar off even as many as the Lord our God shall call."
(Acts 2:38-39)

The day that this all took place, is recorded in my heart and mind. It is my testimony.

CHAPTER FIVE: RECEVING WHAT WAS MINE

CHAPTER FIVE: RECEVING WHAT WAS MINE

There I was, all set to get in the baptismal pool and be baptized in the name of Jesus.

"I beseech you therefore, brethren by the mercies of God that ye present your bodies, a living sacrifice, holly acceptable unto God, which is your reasonable service, and be not conformed to this world: but be ye transformed by the renewing of your mind that ye may prove what is that good and acceptable and perfect will of God." (Romans 12:1-2)

I had no reservations about what I was doing I got in the pool and the minister that was to baptize me said a prayer for me, and then baptized me in the name of Jesus Christ, not in the name of the

Father, Son and The Holy Ghost because, all three of them are one.

"Neither is there salvation in any other: for there is none other name under heaven given among men, whereby we must be saved."
(Acts 4:12)

When the minister lifted me up from completely emerged under the water I began to give God the highest praise, which is Hallelujah. After a few minutes they led me out of the pool, took me back into the alter room, where I began to just praise the Lord and wait to be endued with power from on high. Just as they that waited on the day of Pentecost.

"And when the day of Pentecost was fully come, they were all with one accord in one place. And suddenly there came a sound from heaven as of a rushing mighty wind

and it filled all the house where they were sitting And there appeared unto them cloven tongues like as of fire, and sat upon each of them. And they were all filled with the Holy Ghost, and began to speak with other tongues, as the spirit gave them utterance."
(Acts 2:1-4)

Just like in the bible days God is doing it the same way……

As I continued to give God the highest praise, In my heart and mind I was saying Lord I love you, Lord please forgive me for anything that I have done that was not pleasing to you. While I was thinking those thoughts, I was speaking from my mouth Hallelujah, this went on with so much intensity and anticipation until I began to feel really tired in my body and I was about to just stop.

The minister that baptized me came into the alter room and told me to hold on and to just press my way, he told me that thinking I was too tired to go on was only a distraction from the adversary. He began to share his experience with me about how the adversary tried to make him feel the same way when he had made up his mind that he wanted to be born again. He really encouraged my heart and I continued to press on.

The Lord said in his word that he would never leave you or forsake you. I believe that is why he sent his minister to encourage my heart that I would not leave that church that day the same way I came in. Thank you Lord.

I continued to praise God with my heart, mind, body and soul, all of a sudden there was a light in my mind that had surfaced out of total darkness. I began to follow that beam of light with my body. Where ever the beam of light went I would follow it, it was

A BEAM OF LIGHT
IN A
DARK PLACE

"For thou wilt light my candle: the Lord my god will enlighten my darkness."
(Psalm 18:28)

The just shall live by faith. Religion is not salvation; you are not saved until you receive salvation. You can do it your way when you are out in the world, but when you truly want to be saved, you have to do it Gods way I followed, and followed, and followed, that beam of light, then suddenly my body quicken like an electric jolt, the darkness became a brilliant light that over took my very being, It was the most brilliant bright that I had ever looked upon. When God revealed that beam of light in my heart and mind, I felt as though God had sent a search light out for my soul to be found.

As far away as I was from walking with the Lord, in spite of myself, He sent His love light out for me. It went deep down pass all my faults and found me poor in spirit and all undone. He never made me feel that I was so dirty that there was no hope for me, but with that beam of light he led me to life eternal.

When you are helpless, meaning you've done all that you could do, you need God. My Hallelujah's changed to another language. It was then that I began to speak in other tongues as the spirit of the Lord gave utterance I continued to speak and it was the most exhilarating, spiritual, sweet, comforting and loving experience I have ever felt in my entire life. It was my one on one experience with God It was my testimony that I had been with the Lord. It was my blessed assurance that Jesus was mine. It was my record that had been recorded in the very front of the files in my heart.

"I HAD BEEN BORN AGAIN" HALLELUJAH

"And he that keepeth His Commandments dwelleth in Him and He in him. And hereby we know that He abideth in us by the spirit which He hath given us."
(1st John 3:24)

I have never known such a sense of satisfaction. Words cannot gratify the peace, comfort and love that I was feeling and only those who had been born again could fully understand the love that had been sheded abroad in my heart by the

Holy Ghost. What did I need to do to continue on this way?

CHAPTER SIX: KEEPING WHAT IS MINE

CHAPTER SIX: KEEPING WHAT IS MINE

Until you come to the realization of who Jesus is you will be walking around in darkness, not even knowing that there is a marvelous light available to you that will lead you to life eternal.

It is very surprising to learn that there is a more excellent way of life then what this world has to offer. All we have to do is focus on Gods will for us, and not our own, not what we can acquire in this life with our great wisdom and knowledge that we have bestowed upon ourselves. It's not this world riches, silver and gold cannot buy what the King of glory has prepared for us.

The life that God has prepared is not for a season, it doesn't just fade away with unpopularity or time, its life everlasting. When we find our way in Christ, we will find that His word is as recorded in Heb. 4:12

"For the word of God is quick, and Powerful, and sharper than any two edge sword, piercing even to the dividing asunder of soul and spirit, and of the joints and marrow, and is a discerner of the thoughts and intents of the heart."

I latched on to my new found love Jesus Christ and began to associate myself with His people. I went to prayer meetings and bible class and on Sunday I went to Sunday school then morning service, and evening service. There I would learn how God was working in His people's lives just as He was in the bible days.

There is a healing and learning process in the testimonies of the saints, and how the Lord was always with them through their trials and tribulations. They spoke proven words of how the Lord always brought them out with a mighty stretched out hand and how He would put no more on you then you could bare. I picked up my cross and I began my walk with Jesus. There is a hymn that says, "What a fellowship, what a joy divine leaning on the everlasting arm."

That hymn became more than just a song to me; it became real and active in my heart and in my life. The more I began to know my Lord and Savior, the more I desired to walk with Him.

The more He showed me His word was true and I could look for His promises to come to pass, the more "FAITH" I began to have in Him.

I began experiencing Gods delivering power in my life. As I had mentioned in chapter four, whenever I tried to stand before people to speak in any capacity, I would always be over taken by this spirit of fear that just left me in a trembling state. The first thing that the Lord delivered me from was that spirit of fear.

Today with a great measure of holy boldness I can go before people and speak God's word with authority. What a mighty God we serve. Just as God has inspired men to write His word, He has inspired us to walk in His power. God has not given us a spirit of fear, but of power and love and a sound mind. I am a living witness that Gods promises are real.

CHAPTER SEVEN: MY EXCEEDING AND GREAT REWARD

CHAPTER SEVEN: MY EXCEEDING AND GREAT REWARD

As I continued my walk with God. I learned that when the Lord blesses you with the gift of the Holy Ghost, He also imparts gifts for the edifying of the church. In due season He revealed to me what some of my gifts were.

Before I was saved by God's grace, I had a flair for poetry. After the Holy Ghost comes power. The Lord enhanced my ability to write poetry and writings, usually on a personal level about a specific individual.

In 1995, five years after the Lord so graciously saved me, I was called to the ministry. What being called to the ministry means, is that the Lord impresses upon your heart and mind that there is a particular work that He desires for you to do, that

His word may continue to go forward and not return unto Him void.

When the Lord calls you to do a work for Him, know with assurance that it is the greatest honor that can be bestowed upon anyone. It's also a blessing and a privilege No one has the right to decline, but it is done so often. How frightening is that? My calling was to preach His word to a lost and dying world, and to encourage His people whom He had already saved.

In 1998, the Lord used one of his earthen vessels to open a door for me to begin to teach His word, I love teaching it helps you to grow in the Lord and it is what His people need most of all to continue to walk with Him. Just as you train up a child in the way that they should go and they will not depart from it. When you teach Gods people in the way that they should go they will become strong and established in God's word, just like a tree planted by the water they will not be moved

"Looking for that blessed hope,
And glorious appearing of the
Great God and our Savior Jesus
Christ;"
(Titus 2:13)

When I scale the archives of my heart Jesus is on every file................

With every step of this walk He's walked with me every mile...............

With His precious gift I have been endowed....................................

Oh to be in His presence is a sought after tranquil peace....
A peace of joy and comfort so rewarding And fulfilling, yet only He can release..................................
To know the Savior for yourself

Is an experience not a soul should miss…………………………........

It's life giving and eternally rewarding
So full of only God given happiness……….

To whom much is given, much is required. The saints of God have work to do.

"Go ye therefore, and teach all nations, baptizing them in the Name of The Father, and of The Son, and of The Holy Ghost: Teaching them to observe all things whatsoever I have commanded you: and lo, I am with you always, even unto the end of the world."
(St. Matt. 28:19-20)

CHAPTER EIGHT: FAITH

CHAPTER EIGHT: FAITH

In putting this book together, the enemy fought me very hard. He continually tried to have me to think nothing was right and everything was wrong. For a moment I began to feel as though the ability to even write a book was out of my league and I might as well give up trying. Sometimes the enemy will try and plant doubt, feelings of inadequacy and incapability of achievement. We cannot allow what you have not to hinder what you do have.

I know beyond knowing that by the power that has been vested in me, my knowledge is as large as my Lord and saviour allows it to be. He is my shepherd, and I am His sheep.

"The Lord is my shepherd; I shall not want.
He maketh me to lie down in green pastures: He leadeth me besides the still waters. He restoreth my soul. He leadeth me in the path of righteousness for His name's sake. Yea, though I walk through the valley of the shadow of death, I will fear no evil: for thou art with me; thy rod and thy staff they comfort me. Thou preparest a table before me in the presence of mine enemies: thou anointest my head with oil; my cup runneth over. Surely goodness and mercy shall follow me all the days of my life: and I will dwell in the house of the Lord forever."
(Psalms 23)

When you are a solider in the army of the Lord no weapon formed against you shall prosper. The Lord is able to give you strength that will carry you through anything that He has assigned for you to do. Jesus will strengthen your mind, your heart, and remove any fear or doubt that has come upon you. In this precious walk with Jesus you have to walk by "FAITH" and not by sight. Things that look too hard to try are not too hard when you know Jesus.

A mirage looks real until you're right upon it, and then you will see that it was actually nothing, as a matter of a fact it is not even there. When you are walking in Gods strength and by His spirit you can walk in the unknown because, Jesus holds your hand. God truly cares for your soul and His desire for you is to go out and tell the world that He is alive. The very best way that we can tell someone that has an ear to hear and eyes to see, is through the life that we talk and live.

We have to walk the life that we talk about. We have to display what we say. It is my "Faith" in God that has brought me to this point in my life. I have had to weather a few storms and hurdle a few stumbling blocks. I have had to learn to fast and pray, run to the altar for renewed determination and strength.

Thank God for the power that He has vested in me.

The God that I serve is real, He is not a God made by hands. The God of my salvation is the God that came down from His glorious throne from on high (heaven). He walked this earth for over 33 years, preaching and teaching the way to eternal life, The Kingdom of God.

He died a sinner's death on Calvary's Cross, that we might have life. And that more abundantly." His Pain Our Gain"

What manner of love is this? Jesus is alive, He is alive in me and for those who have not yet come to know Him in the power of His resurrection, He can become alive in you.

He rose on the third day with all power in His hand and death could not keep Him in the grave.

My Lord and Savior Jesus Christ is alive, and He is coming back for His bride, the church. When the final hour has come will you be able to stand?

> "He which testifieth these things saith surly I come quickly Amen. Even so come Lord Jesus"
> (Rev. 22:20)

…….THE END…….

FAITH: THE POEM

FAITH: THE POEM

No man is an island everyone needs a strong hand…….
When strength has grown weak the power of God will stand…..
When every help imaginable has been exhausted………….
Put on your FAITH and know that God can…………………
His ability surpasses all human understanding
Because, the world is in His hand……….
FAITH is what will began your walk and
FAITH will take you to the end……….
any help that you receive from any man on this earth is all in Gods Holy anointed plan………….

…..FAITH…..

      Forever
      Alive
      IN
      TRUE
      HOPE

"Commit thy way unto the Lord
Trust also in Him; and He shall
Bring it to pass."
(Psalms 37:5)

ABOUT THE AUTHOR
DAINAH FELTON

ABOUT THE AUTHOR

Dainah Felton was born and raised in Detroit, Michigan to the parents of Jesse and Elizabeth L. Garth. She is a minister called to preach the word of God. She is an active member of her church, The Pentecostal Church of Jesus Christ, located in Eastpointe, Michigan, where her present Pastor is Elder Keith L. Spiller Sr. Her husband Elder Timothy O. Felton Sr. is Assistant Pastor.

She has four children, Timothy Jr., Patrick, Pamela, and Kysha. six grandchildren, Jo'von, Kori, Taylor, Ky're, Lauryn, and Nia. And one great grandson, Geremiah. Dainah has two brothers, Robert and Jeff, and three sisters, Sylvia, Katherine and Tanya. She also has two sisters in the Great State of Ohio, Willadean and Dorothy.

"I will bless the Lord at all times: His praise shall continually be in my mouth. My soul shall make her boast in the Lord: the humble shall hear thereof, and be glad. O magnify the Lord with me, and let us exalt His name together. I sought the Lord, and He heard me, and delivered me from all my fears."
(Psalm 34 1- 4)

"I Bless Your Name Lord"

CONTACT INFORMATION

Dainah Garth Felton
Email: <u>dainahfelton@gmail.com</u>

www.ingramcontent.com/pod-product-compliance
Ingram Content Group UK Ltd.
Pitfield, Milton Keynes, MK11 3LW, UK
UKHW041413180426
11947UKWH00007B/100